JOHNNY CASH

A Life from Beginning to End

Copyright © 2022 by Hourly History.

D1082566

Table of Contents

Introduction

Johnny Cash began life in the poverty-stricken confines of Kingsland, Arkansas, the son of Ray and Carrie Cash. Born on February 26, 1932, Johnny was preceded in birth by his older brothers Roy and Jack, as well as his older sister Margaret. He would also have three younger siblings—Reba, Joanne, and Tommy.

At the time of Johnny Cash's birth, the United States and much of the rest of the world was locked in the grip of what was known as the Great Depression. World economies were in a tailspin, and where Johnny and his family lived in Arkansas, there simply weren't enough jobs to go around. Johnny's father, Ray, had to make an effort to find what little work there was and became a jack of all trades as a result. He gained temporary employment working at sawmills, laboring for railroad companies, toiling away on farms, and a wide variety of other odd jobs. When he wasn't able to gain traditional modes of employment, he wasn't above catching rabbits and squirrels, bringing them home and butchering them himself just to have something on the dinner table.

Ray Cash didn't even have proper transportation, and like many down on their luck in those days, he often hitched a ride on trains to get around. He didn't buy a train ticket but simply jumped on the back of a train car as it was passing by. Ray had apparently made his train-hopping so routine that little Johnny didn't give it a second thought. As Johnny himself would later recall, "Our house was right on the railroad tracks—and one of my earliest memories is of seeing him jump out of a moving boxcar and roll down the ditch in front of our door."

It was certainly a hard-knock life, but, seen through the lens of the Great Depression-era, Johnny Cash never thought much of it.

Chapter One

Early Life on the Family Farm

"I learned to throw a bowie knife and kill a jack rabbit at forty yards, not for the sport but because I was hungry."

—Johnny Cash

In the early 1930s, President Franklin D. Roosevelt set in motion several government programs to provide some relief to those who were hit hardest by the economic downturn of the Great Depression. Johnny's father Ray applied for one of these programs and filled out an application in which he had to list off just about every detail of his financial and home life before sending it off to Washington, D.C. His application was accepted, and as a result, he and his family were granted some land on government property allocated in Dyess, Arkansas. Here, government housing had been built upon 16,000 acres of reclaimed swampland.

The Cash family arrived at Dyess in the spring of 1935 when Johnny was three years old. Their new home was officially known as "House 266" in government records, but for young Johnny Cash and his family, it was nothing short of the promised land. The house may have lacked plumbing and electricity, but it did boast five rooms and a chicken coop. It also had 20 acres of surrounding land in which the family could grow their own food. Johnny had a place to lay his head, and the chickens and surrounding crops provided regular meals—for a family that was practically starving at the time, this was indeed a step up.

The families at Dyess also benefited from government-run health care that provided routine doctor's visits. For many who had never seen a doctor in their life, it was a true blessing. Even so, life wasn't easy. The family was hit hard in January of 1937 when the homestead was hit with a terrible spate of flooding, which was worsened by the fact that the houses were built on reclaimed swampland. It was so bad that the family had to vacate their home. By the time they returned, they found everything ruined. Their crops were destroyed, snakes had made their way into the barn, and whatever chickens had survived had laid eggs all over the place. The family worked hard to straighten everything out and were soon able to get their lives back on track.

From this experience, Johnny Cash would later write the song called "Five Feet High and Rising." The song had Johnny casting himself back into the role of a child, asking, "How high's the water, mama?" to which his mother responded, "Two feet high and rising." He then asked his dad, "How high's the water, papa?" who confirmed what the mother said, "She said— it's two feet high and rising."

The song then progresses with the situation getting steadily worse, at one point describing the desolation of the farm, "Well, the hives are gone, I've lost my bees. The chickens are sleeping in the willow trees. Cow's in water up past her knees. Three feet high and rising." By the end of the song, the water level is up to five feet, and the family has to be evacuated. As Cash sings it, "Well, the rails are washed out north of town. We got to head for higher ground. We can't come back till the water goes down. Five feet high and rising."

Following this disaster, Johnny Cash began his first year of school in 1938. At this tender age, he also started to work the fields with his parents and older siblings. Just about every day after school, Johnny could be found laboring away in the cotton fields. It was perhaps in these fields that Johnny first became accustomed to humming and singing a tune to make the toil of his labor a little less tedious.

Around this time, Cash also began to sing in his local church. The church featured a full worship band with guitar, mandolin, and banjos, and Johnny very much enjoyed the music he was exposed to every Sunday morning. Johnny's father, on the other hand, didn't have much of a taste for music, often expressing his opinion that the kids would be better off working than wasting time singing.

Despite Ray's misgivings, Johnny's mother was a big supporter of developing musical taste in her children, and she encouraged them to take part in music whenever they could. Johnny Cash took full advantage. He would later recall, "We sang in the house, on the porch, everywhere." For Johnny, singing was like breathing, and he would keep this love for music for the rest of his days.

Chapter Two

The Death of His Brother

"There's no way around grief and loss: you can dodge all you want, but sooner or later you just have to go into it, through it, and, hopefully, come out the other side. The world you find there will never be the same as the world you left."

—Johnny Cash

By the early 1940s, the Cash household had changed tremendously. With America's entrance into World War II, Johnny's older brother Roy was drafted and sent overseas. Roy was often the leader of the children and almost a father-type figure. With his oldest brother gone, Johnny became closer to the second oldest Cash son— Jack. Jack was a hard worker with good character and often spoke of his intention of one day seeking a profession as a Baptist preacher. Johnny greatly respected his brother and looked up to him. Having that said, Johnny Cash's world would be shaken to its core when one Saturday, on May 12, 1944, the unthinkable happened.

Jack, thinking the family needed some extra money, was busying himself at a local workshop sawing fence posts. Tragically, the mechanized saw he used had not been properly safeguarded, and Jack accidentally fell right on top of it, slicing his abdomen wide open. It was a terrible injury that would prove fatal, with Jack passing away about a week later, aged only 15.

Johnny had been out fishing when his father when the local preacher found him and told him the news. Casting his fishing pole to the side, Johnny jumped into the preacher's car and headed to the hospital where his brother had been taken. It was a terrible scene when Jack finally passed on May 20, yet there was some light to be found in all of this darkness. It would later be recalled that the dying Jack looked to his mother and asked her if she could hear the angels that were gathered around. Jack then claimed that he could hear them singing. Jack, through his anguish, was suddenly at peace as he tried to describe to his family what he was seeing. Jack told them, "It's so wonderful—and what a beautiful place I'm going." He passed away shortly thereafter.

Cash would later reflect that when his brother died, he felt like a piece of himself had perished as well. According to Johnny, it was in the midst of this turmoil of deep emotion that his songwriting career truly began. Cash would later recall that he was just "trying to put down what I was feeling" in the aftermath of his brother's passing. The guilt he felt was only compounded by his father, who blamed Johnny for not being there when Jack was injured.

Also around this time, Johnny became friends with a boy at his school named Pete Barnhill, who had his own flattop guitar. He and Pete would hang out, listen to the radio, and try to sing and play along to their favorite tunes. As Cash perfected his singing voice with Pete, his mother took notice. She sincerely believed that her son had some rather incredible talent when it came to music and even got a second job doing laundry to pay for music lessons for Johnny. This led Cash to have sessions with a young instructor by the name of LaVanda Mae Fielder in the neighboring town of Lepanto, Arkansas.

Fielder was a proper, classically trained instructor, and rather than having Cash belt out the hits like he was accustomed to, she had him sing classic standards designed to improve his technique. At one point, however, she had him deviate away from the standards for a moment and asked him to sing something he wanted to sing. Upon being given this suggestion, Cash immediately burst into a rendition of Hank Williams' song, "Long Gone Lonesome Blues."

Upon hearing Cash's powerful, raw rendition, the music teacher was impressed. She even advised him to stop taking voice lessons because she believed Johnny was best in his own raw element. She then gave him the parting advice of "don't let me or anyone else change the way you sing." Cash listened to the words of his instructor and, to his mother's chagrin, never took formal music lessons again. Instead, he perfected his own self-taught style of haunting yet harmonious singing, which the whole world would one day come to know.

Chapter Three

Service in the Korean War

"How well I have learned that there is no fence to sit on between heaven and hell. There is a deep, wide gulf, a chasm, and in that chasm is no place for any man."

—Johnny Cash

During his high school days, his peers would recall Johnny Cash as a boy with a sensitive streak. He always seemed to be in tune with his feelings, which often stood in sharp contrast with his more rough and tumble classmates. Most of the boys were focused on sports and having a good time, while Johnny often surprised others with his deep philosophical views.

Cash's school had a low graduation rate, with many opting to drop out and work rather than finish earning their diploma. There were only 13 pupils left who managed to step across the stage when Johnny graduated in 1950. The fact that Johnny Cash was among the few to stick it out to the end was a testament to his tenacity and bright mind.

Upon graduating, Cash knew that he wanted to leave Dyess to pursue bigger and better things. However, like many young farm boys in those days, he just wasn't sure how to get off the farm. His first attempt to leave Dyess behind failed miserably. He hopped on a bus and headed to Pontiac, Michigan. Here, he got a job at a car factory and was put up in a crowded boarding house when he wasn't on the assembly line. Cash would later recall how miserable it was. He was elbow to elbow "with men who drank and cussed and carried on more than my tender young country sensibilities could stand." Unable to tolerate life in Pontiac, Cash quit and returned home after just three weeks. Back home, he then tried his luck at a nearby margarine plant but found the low pay and poor working conditions unbearable.

It was while Johnny Cash was in this quandary and crossroads as to what to do with his life that the U.S. found itself locked in a new conflict known as the Korean War. North Korea had just invaded South Korea, and U.S. troops were being called in to push them back. Like many young men at the time, Cash figured the military was about as good a ticket away from home as any. Having decided to join up, he went to a recruiting station and signed on with the Air Force. He later explained the decision as being simply because he liked the image of flying.

Johnny Cash then became an officially enlisted man on July 7, 1950. Shortly thereafter, he was put on a train and sent off to Lackland Air Base in San Antonio, Texas to start basic training. Cash had cited his main reason for joining as being he liked the idea of flying, but not everyone who joins the Air Force becomes a pilot, and neither did Cash. Instead, he was fast-tracked into a program to work as a radio operator, tasked with the transcription of broadcasts.

After undergoing a few months of training, Cash was eventually enlisted with a unit called the Twelfth Radio Squadron Mobile, or "RSM" for short. He was subsequently shipped back to Texas—this time to Brooks Air Force Base, where he trained for an additional eight weeks. It was here, while he was on leave and hanging out at a local roller-skating rink, that he met the woman who would become his first wife.

She was 17-year-old Vivian Liberto. As soon as Cash laid eyes on her, he was compelled to go over and strike up a conversation. Vivian, for her part, must have been just as easily charmed by this soldier, and the two were soon dating. Their courtship would be a brief one, however, since Cash was soon shipped off to a U.S. base in Landsberg, Germany, where he would be set to work intercepting communications from the Soviet Union. The young warrior wouldn't fail to write his new love though, and Vivian was faithful to him as well, never failing to respond back.

Cash, meanwhile, proved himself to be quite good at decrypting the Morse code messages that were being intercepted from the Russians. So good, in fact, that he received the promotion of staff sergeant in a short amount of time. When his hands weren't on the dials of his radio, Cash was most likely singing and playing guitar. During this period, he got together with some like-minded servicemen and even started his own band, a group that was rather comically dubbed the Landsberg Barbarians. This was apparently in comic reference to the base's local newspaper, which was called *The Landsberg Bavarian*. Johnny wrote his own songs too, including a religious-themed piece called "Belshazzar" and a song called "Hey, Porter."

It was while in Germany that Cash also first got a taste for alcohol. Germany is, of course, famous for beer drinking, and most restless young servicemen couldn't resist doing a bit of carousing at local pubs and bars while staying in Germany. As Cash would later recall, "I took a part in most everything else that goes along with drunkenness that last year in Germany."

Nevertheless, even throughout his bouts of periodic drunkenness, Johnny was sure to attend military chapel services, pray, and read his Bible. As Cash would later describe his penchant for engaging in both religion and mischief in one of his most famous songs, it was in Landsberg that he first learned to "walk the line." Interestingly enough, he also found himself walking the line with his relationship with Vivian.

In more than one letter, Cash wrote to his sweetheart back home and confided in her that he had been involved with other girls in Germany. Even in his confession, he assured her that his heart was still faithful to her, and he urged her to be the same way. In a letter dated from 1952, Cash explained, "Darling, those girls don't mean a thing to me. You should know that. I just see them one night and never see them again. Baby, I'd trade 100 of girls like that for one kiss from you."

Some might judge Vivian as gullible for believing Cash, but she did. Furthermore, she made sure she was faithful to him, refraining from any serious involvement until he returned. Cash rewarded her faithfulness in February of 1953 by mailing her an engagement ring.

Chapter Four

Cash's First Wife

"All your life, you will be faced with a choice.
You can choose love or hate . . . I choose love."

—Johnny Cash

Johnny Cash was honorably discharged from the military on July 3, 1954, and arrived at an airport in Memphis, Tennessee the following day. That Independence Day holiday proved to be a happy one, as his family, as well as his fiancée Vivian Liberto, greeted him at the airport. It was Vivian that Johnny ran to first, and as soon as the couple embraced, it was hard to pry them apart. They hugged and kissed for so long that it wasn't until Johnny Cash's usually stern and reserved father delivered the wisecrack, "Vivian! You're going to eat him up!" that they let go. Bursting into laughter, the happy couple finally relented, and Johnny went on to greet his parents, siblings, and other relatives who hadn't seen him in three years.

After landing in Memphis, Cash and company headed back to his hometown of Dyess, where he showed Vivian around while simultaneously showing his new fiancée off to all of his old friends and acquaintances. After this sightseeing tour of Dyess, he and Vivian drove to San Antonio, Texas, where Johnny had the hard work of convincing Vivian's parents that he was marriage material.

Initially, her parents were skeptical. They thought Cash was a nice enough guy, but due to their Catholic upbringing, they were not too eager to see their daughter marry a Protestant. One reassurance for Vivian's father Tom was the fact that Johnny agreed to marry Vivian in a Catholic Church and promised to raise any subsequent children he might have with her in the Catholic faith. To hear such words of dedication out of the month of this young soldier impressed Tom, and he finally gave his blessing to the union.

The only trouble was, after Cash's discharge from the military, he was left unemployed. He could hardly marry Vivian without a job, so he began to ask around about any opportunities for work. A friend recommended that he check with a local appliance shop in Memphis, called the Home Equipment Company. He ended up getting a job as an appliance salesman. Feeling reassured that he had a job lined up, Johnny Cash then found an apartment in Memphis that he and Vivian could call home. It was a cheap little hole in the wall that Johnny acquired with what was left over from his earnings in the Air Force, but it would have to suffice until they could save up some money.

In the midst of all this preparation, Cash also made sure that he indulged his love for music. Utilizing the G.I. Bill, which paid for the schooling of veterans, he signed on at the local Keegan's School of Broadcasting in Memphis so that he could take courses geared towards becoming a radio broadcaster.

Johnny was pleased with the direction of his life and excited for the future when he and Vivian finally got married at St. Ann's Catholic Church on August 7, 1954. Presiding over the wedding was Vivian's uncle, Father Vincent Liberto. After the wedding, the newly christened Mr. and Mrs. Cash attended a brief reception with family before heading off on their own to Palestine, Texas, where they would have their honeymoon.

Right around the time of their honeymoon, Johnny's musical ears would perk up to a brand-new sound that was hitting the airwaves. That summer, a young man by the name of Elvis Presley came out with an exciting new sound that had been dubbed rock n' roll. Elvis had come from a similar background as Cash. He too was southern, and he too had been born in abject poverty, with only a love for music to sustain him. The affinity with this new star was almost immediate, and when Johnny Cash learned that Elvis was a recording artist based out of Memphis for a record label called Sun Records, he almost went through the roof. Immediately Cash thought to himself—if Elvis could do it, then he could too.

Chapter Five

Meeting Elvis Presley

"Elvis was so good. Every show I did with him, I never missed the chance to stand in the wings and watch. We all did. He was that charismatic."

—Johnny Cash

By the late summer of 1954, Johnny Cash began to play music with a couple of guys that his brother Roy had introduced him to—Marshall Grant and Luther Perkins. Marshall and Luther worked as car mechanics to make a living, but like Cash, their true passion was in music. Both Marshall and Luther played guitar and sang their own songs, and as Cash would later recall, as soon as he got together with them, they would "sing and play until the early hours of the morning, night after night."

Cash was a young family man with a wife and a child on the way, but he hadn't given up on his dream of music and continued to pursue it every chance he got. As he and his friends perfected their craft, the group started to move towards a more powerful sound by having Perkins play lead on electric guitar while Grant picked up the bass. This dynamic pair would henceforth be known as the Tennessee Two and the primary backing band of Johnny Cash.

After getting down a few songs, the group played their first gig at a local church in Memphis. This was then followed by a performance at a local fundraiser for a local man and friend of Marshall Grant's by the name of Ralph Johnson. Ralph, an avid powerboat racer, had been recently injured in a boat crash, and the proceeds of the concert went to pay for his medical bills.

The first time the group actually made money for themselves was when they played on the back of a flatbed truck as part of an advertising campaign for Hurst Motor Company, a gig which earned them fifty dollars to split amongst each other. They also managed to get some live airtime, playing on Saturday broadcasts of KWEM, which was sponsored by Johnny's day job with the Home Equipment Company.

Cash and the Tennessee Two were really getting some recognition now, but in order to go all the way, they knew that they would have to get some studio time and make some recordings of their own. It was for this reason that Cash once again turned his eyes toward the Memphis-based record company that had given rise to his hero Elvis, Sun Records.

Johnny Cash first met Elvis on September 9, 1954, when Elvis was performing at the opening of a new drug store. It certainly doesn't sound very glamorous—and it wasn't. Elvis Presley and his backup band were playing in the back of a flatbed truck just as Cash and the Tennessee Two had in the past. Even though Elvis was a rising talent with his hist "That's All Right" getting frequent airplay on radio stations, he had not yet become a household name in 1954. Even so, once Johnny Cash saw Presley in person, he was even more convinced that Elvis was going to become very big, very soon. As Cash would later recall, "The first time I saw Elvis, singing from a flatbed truck at a Katz drugstore opening on Lamar Avenue, two or three hundred people, mostly teenage girls, had come to see him."

After navigating his way through Elvis' growing crowd of female admirers, Johnny Cash managed to walk up to him and introduce himself. Cash was forthright with his admiration, admitting to Elvis that he was a fan of his music.

Elvis, grateful for the praise, asked Johnny to attend his next gig at a place called the Eagle's Nest. Sure enough, Cash was in attendance and was once again blown away by Presley's star quality. Cash left that gig more determined than ever to break out into music on his own.

Cash knew that if he wanted to make a name for himself like Elvis was doing, he needed to have some recordings under his belt. Thus, at this time, he began to turn his attention to Sun Records, the Memphis record company that had helped launch Presley's career.

At the advice of one of Presley's bandmates, Cash took the leap and dialed up the owner of Sun Records, Sam Phillips. He was informed by the secretary that Mr. Phillips was not in the office. In a strange way, Johnny Cash was actually relieved that Phillips wasn't there. In the meantime, Cash began to seriously refine the songs that he played with his band.

Eventually, Cash did indeed get Phillips on the phone, but in Cash's own words "he turned me down flat." Johnny Cash was growing increasingly frustrated at this point and decided to take matters into his own hands. He did so, one fine day in November of 1954, by going to Sun Records in person and sitting right down on the front step, determined to get Sam Phillips to give him the time of day.

Sure enough, Phillips arrived on the scene to find Cash planted right in front of the studio. He was greeted with the words, "I'm John Cash. I'm the one that's been calling. And if you'd listen to me, I believe you'll be glad you did." It was Cash's dogged determination that finally got Phillips' attention, and he finally agreed to allow Cash and the Tennessee Two to audition for him.

Fortunately, Phillips liked what he heard. He appreciated the unique sound of Johnny Cash's voice, but he didn't have much of an appetite for the gospel songs Cash primarily played in those days. Being about as forthright as he could, he informed the group, "If you come up with something original, something that's not gospel, I'd like to hear you again."

Johnny Cash and his wife Vivian were, in the meantime, finding their tiny apartment to be just a little too crowded for their style. Vivian was pregnant, and Johnny was also worried that she might slip and fall having to climb the stairs. He knew they needed to find something better. It was while Johnny was working a shift on the floor of the Home Equipment Company that he came across a customer who offered to rent him a more spacious duplex that she and her husband were renting nearby. The rent was cheap and even when Johnny was a little short, his kind landlords allowed him to get by on their hospitality alone.

While all this was going down, Johnny Cash and his bandmates were searching for some original tunes that they could present to Phillips at Sun Records. This search had Johnny refining an old song he had begun crafting long ago, called "Hey, Porter." Another song that Johnny Cash was developing at the very same time was one that would later become one of his greatest hits, entitled "Folsom Prison Blues." To Johnny's chagrin, Phillips wasn't interested in it at the time and insisted that he stick with "Hey, Porter."

At any rate, it was on the strength of this song that Phillips would eventually agree to give the band studio time. So it was, in May of 1955, right around the time that Johnny's first child, Rosanne, was born, that he and the Tennessee Two belted out their first recordings. They ended up recording both "Hey, Porter" and a B-side track Cash came up with called "Cry, Cry, Cry."

Phillips liked the originality of "Cry, Cry, Cry" and decided to make it the first single to be released. Once it hit the airwaves, listeners agreed. Soon Cash and the Tennessee Two could be heard on radio stations all throughout the Southern United States. It was on the strength of this airplay that Cash and the Tennessee Two began to receive regular concert bookings, and when Cash learned that he would be making about $30 a night for his efforts, he was more than ready to quit his day job. It may not seem like much today, but for Cash, who couldn't even make that much in a week as a salesman, $30 a night was a fortune.

With the promise of a regular income at the ready, Johnny Cash was all set to become a musician full time.

Chapter Six

Cash's First Hit Song

"Success is having to worry about every damn thing in the world, except money."

—Johnny Cash

After receiving significant play on the radio in the summer of 1955, Johnny Cash and the Tennessee Two played across a wide swath of the surrounding area of southwestern Tennessee and northwestern Arkansas. At these concerts, they would typically perform their two new singles as well as a smattering of gospel tunes and a few pop songs. It was at this point that Cash would begin to develop a bit of a rivalry with Elvis, who was a sensation in the South but had not yet broken through to the rest of the country.

Both artists played at a concert at the venue in Memphis called the Overton Park Shell on August 5, 1955—an open-air stage in the middle of Memphis' Overton Park. The big draw was Elvis, but Johnny Cash wasn't far behind, along with 20 other acts that performed for some 4,000 fans gathered at the park. As they were accustomed to doing, when it was time for Cash and the Tennessee Two, they played their two singles which were circulating on the radio. They were called back for an encore, and when they did so, they decided to perform a riveting version of "Folsom Prison Blues."

This concert would be viewed as the moment that Johnny Cash hit it big. However, there was one person among the thousands of people packed together at Overton Park who wasn't too happy about this newfound success. That person was Johnny Cash's wife, Vivian. Although she wanted him to succeed, seeing how all of the young women clamored for Elvis that day, Vivian for the first time began to become afraid for her marriage. She knew that it would only take one of those thousands of adoring fans to tempt her husband and possibly lead him astray. She couldn't help but fear for the future of her and Johnny Cash's relationship.

Johnny and Elvis' relationship was also about to drastically change just as Presley was about to break out onto the national scene. Prior to becoming a national superstar, Elvis and Johnny were both managed by a popular local Memphis disc jockey by the name of Bob Neal. But as he was about to step onto the national stage, a promoter who went by the name of Colonel Tom Parker began to pull Elvis away.

Around this time, both Johnny Cash and Elvis Presley went on tour in Texas. They played the same venues, but Colonel Parker managed to drum up more interest in Elvis than Cash could muster. Just prior to an Elvis concert, Parker would go around town handing out tickets to young women, telling them that the tickets were free of charge on the condition that they all shout "We want Elvis!" These young ladies fulfilled their part of the bargain and were indeed screaming Elvis' name throughout the performance.

Cash and the Tennessee Two meanwhile often received mixed reactions. Some enjoyed their performance, but others didn't quite know what to make of it. Cash would get better traction after December 15, 1955, when Sun Records put out the single for "Folsom Prison Blues." The song, which speaks of an inmate stuck in prison, was certainly unique. No one had ever heard anything quite like it before. Yet, the realness of the music hit home, and it was soon in high demand. The following month in January of 1956, a 24-year-old Johnny Cash was given his first royalty check in the amount of $6,000. Johnny Cash had never seen so much money in his life.

The song "Folsom Prison Blues" would go on to become a top-ten hit on the country charts, and by the spring of 1956, Cash was ready to record more music. Among the new recordings he rendered was a song called "I Walk the Line." Cash initially played the song as a slow, almost church-like ballad. Sam Phillips encouraged him to play in a livelier tempo, which seemed to change the feel of the song entirely. This song would end up becoming one of Cash's biggest hits, yet incredibly enough, when Cash heard the recording, he thought it was terrible. According to him, he only started to like it because everyone else did. And like it they did—the song rose up to the top of the country music charts.

With the sudden influx of money that all of his royalties provided, Johnny Cash bought his family a big house, a nice car, and generally lavished upon himself and his friends and family all of the good things in life. Since Vivian had just given birth to their second child, Kathy, in April of that year—the timing couldn't have been better. Johnny was now determined to provide for his children all of the things in life that he couldn't have growing up.

Johnny Cash had certainly come a long way since his days living in flooded government housing in Dyess, Arkansas.

Chapter Seven

Struggle with Addiction

"Sometimes I am two people. Johnny is the nice one. Cash causes all the trouble."

—Johnny Cash

Johnny Cash reached yet another milestone in his career on July 7, 1956, when he made an appearance at the Grand Ole Opry. The Grand Ole Opry has long been a staple of the Nashville country music scene, where the greats of the genre have played. Cash performed his latest masterpiece, "I Walk the Line." The song, as well as Cash in general, were well received. Afterward, Cash expressed his gratitude for the opportunity to play for the Opry. He plainly stated, "It's the ambition of every hillbilly singer to reach the Opry in his lifetime."

Cash's performance at the Opry would have even further implications upon his life, for it was here that he would meet the woman who would one day become his second wife, June Carter. June was part of a singing group composed of some of her relatives, simply called the Carter Family. The Carter Family specialized in the regional country-folk music of southwestern Virginia. June was a great singer with natural charisma both on and off the stage, just as Johnny Cash discovered after his concert came to a close.

The two apparently hit off right away, and even though they were both married at the time, a spark went off between them that would never go out. Johnny had even joked with June at the time that someday he would marry her—a jest that his wife Vivian certainly wouldn't have appreciated had she known that it had occurred. Vivian wanted Johnny to stay home with her and the kids, not out galivanting around on stage. Yet Johnny Cash's recent success with singles such as "I Walk the Line" would lead him to engage in even more extensive touring. By December of 1956, he would even take his act all the way to Canada.

His family was growing in the meantime, with Vivian giving birth to their third child together, Cindy, in 1959. Cash would later shoulder a good deal of guilt for being away from his children during their early years, and his non-stop touring and performing was taking a toll not only on his home life but also on his health. Upon returning from the Canada leg of his journey, Cash complained to his friend Ted Freeman, "I'm twenty-six pounds lighter and ten years older. We averaged four hundred and twenty miles per day, and I am tired and sick."

It was his rigorous schedule that would lead Cash to first take amphetamines to stay awake. It wasn't uncommon for performers to turn to drugs like these in order to up their performance. Johnny soon became hooked. The pills took the edge off and gave him greater confidence on stage—it wasn't long before a dependency was developed.

By this point, Cash and his family had moved out to Encino, California, but Johnny wasn't there much to enjoy it with his family. With his newfound drug of choice, he was now almost always on the road. When he was home, he often stayed up all night writing songs. Despite his frequent absences, Johnny and Vivian did manage to have what would be their fourth and last child together, Tara, who was born on August 24, 1961.

Nevertheless, Vivian would later recall how she spent most nights in bed alone, only to wake up and find Cash in the den, hyped up and crafting his latest tunes. Vivian didn't know that much about the drugs that Cash was on, but she knew that such things could not be sustainable. She feared that her husband was bound to crash, and she was right. Marshall Grant would later recall just how out of it Cash could be. He remembered several nights in which the band would go out on stage, and Cash was almost in a daze as if he didn't even know where he was. Yet according to Grant, after the crowd would stand up screaming and hollering, Cash would snap back to reality and run through his hits as if on autopilot.

The drugs that had previously helped Cash perform were beginning to eat away at his sanity, making him increasingly irrational. So irrational, in fact, that he would vent his rage at inanimate objects as if they had feelings—as was the case during one particularly infamous incident in November of 1961 when Cash tried to kick down the door of a club because he thought it was refusing to let him in. Those closest to him knew that Cash was just about ripe for an intervention.

Chapter Eight

Relationship with June Carter

"There's unconditional love there. You hear that phrase a lot but it's real with me and her. She loves me in spite of everything, in spite of myself. She has saved my life more than once."

—Johnny Cash

By the early 1960s, Johnny Cash had become increasingly erratic. He was still a good showman on stage, but offstage he was entirely unpredictable. As band member Marshall Grant described it, Cash could be "one of the greatest human beings" one minute and then "the greatest jerk that ever lived" the next.

The drugs he took to stay awake for days on end were taking their toll. Johnny's wife, his bandmates, and just about everyone else now knew that they had to somehow get him off of the drugs he was hooked on. Out of everyone Cash was acquainted with, it was his old friend June Carter, whom he had met at the Grand Ole Opry all those years ago, who directly intervened on his behalf.

June knew all the signs of a drug addict from musicians that she and the Carter Family had performed with in the past. She knew that Johnny Cash was in a downward spiral, and she became determined to pull him out of it. Although the two were certainly attracted to each other, June was still taken—this time to a second husband by the name of Edwin Nix. Initially, June's primary focus with Johnny Cash wasn't necessarily romance—but rather rehabilitation.

It's said that June Carter and Marshall Grant staged a major intervention in which they forced Cash to detox from the drugs he was taking. They took his pills away from him, tossing them in the nearest toilet. Grant would later recall how they would stay up all night to keep watch over Cash, "just to keep him alive and stop him from hurting anybody."

As June became increasingly involved with Cash's rehabilitation, her and Johnny's relationship began to evolve into something more than a friend helping another friend. Soon an affair developed, but both were careful to keep the situation entirely secret from both their respective spouses and the prying eyes of the public. Johnny Cash especially worried about what such a fling would do to his public image since he had long held the public persona of being a devoted family man. For now, they managed to keep the whole ordeal—both Cash's rehab and his affair—quiet.

Back to his senses, the next major concern for Johnny Cash was to get back in the saddle as it pertained to his music. He hadn't had a hit song in a while and felt like he had fallen off track. June, meanwhile, had just collaborated on a song with singer/songwriter Merle Kilgore called "Ring of Fire." The song was then handed off to June's sister, Anita Carter, who released it as a single in November of 1962. With June's permission, Cash would go on to record his own version, which would be released through his new record company—Columbia Records—in the spring of 1963.

This song, which described love as a burning ring of fire, would become one of Cash's all-time greatest hits. The song would reach the top of the country charts and remain there for nearly two months. Johnny Cash, in the meantime, was becoming less and less discreet about his relationship with June Carter. Along with borrowing her tune for "Ring of Fire," he began to record songs with her and was frequently a special guest for Carter Family studio sessions.

Things then came to a head when Vivian, along with her and Johnny's children, attended a performance of Cash's Hollywood Bowl show and witnessed the closeness of Johnny and June firsthand. She was appalled to see her often cold and distant husband snuggled up next to June. According to Johnny's daughter Kathy's later recollection, "We were standing there waving good-bye to Dad, and he kissed us all, got into his car, and then June jumped into the car right next to him and waved to us. Mom was furious. That was when she started falling apart."

Vivian had good reason to be furious. Although others may have chided her at the time not to be jealous of Cash and Carter since they were fellow musicians who worked together, the chemistry that Johnny and June shared was obvious. This, along with Johnny's complete inattention to Vivian and the family, made it clear to her that she was being replaced. Kathy Cash was old enough to recall the fallout and vividly remembered how when her father did come home, terrible fights would ensue between him and Vivian. Vivian desperately wanted a husband who was serious about his family and who wouldn't spend so much time away with other people. Cash, on the other hand, wasn't willing to change his lifestyle and argued that Vivian was being unreasonable.

At any rate, Cash had fallen head over heels in love with June. He had always liked her, and when she saved him from addiction when no one else could, his love for her grew even stronger. Johnny also felt a kind of kinship with June that he never quite had with Vivian. He and June shared similar life experiences, and he felt that she understood him on a level that Vivian never would. Even though Johnny and Vivian wouldn't officially file for divorce until 1966, the writing was already on the wall.

Chapter Nine

Johnny Cash and the Highwaymen

"When I record somebody else's song, I have to make it my own or it doesn't feel right. I'll say to myself, I wrote this and he doesn't know it!"

—Johnny Cash

As much as June had helped Johnny recover from his abuse of amphetamines, by the fall of 1965, Cash had almost completely relapsed. His mental collapse was on full display in September of that year when he performed on *TheSteve Lawrence Show* on CBS for a segment called "Nashville in New York." Embarrassingly enough, Johnny was so out of it that he found himself completely unable to do the routines that he and his band had rehearsed.

If things weren't bad enough, the following month Cash was busted on narcotics charges. He had been caught bringing drugs into the country from Mexico at El Paso International Airport on October 4. Sliding back into his old habits, Cash had apparently crossed the border to buy a large amount of amphetamines. The bond hearing that Cash was forced to attend turned into a real circus in which an increasingly agitated Cash threatened to kick one photographer's camera out of his hands.

Cash ended up pleading guilty to the charges and received a 30-day suspended sentence, along with a $1,000 fine. Even this brush with the law wasn't enough to get Cash to kick the habit for good, and by the spring of 1966, he was back at it again, as was evidenced in March of that year when Johnny Cash was seen in a drug-induced stupor wandering around on stage during a gig at Toronto's O'Keefe Centre.

Johnny Cash also began to disappear once again. His wife Vivian was used to Johnny being gone for long stretches, but she could usually track him down. Now, she found it increasingly difficult to get a bead on him. Finally fed up with the direction their relationship had taken, Vivian filed for divorce on June 30, 1966. The paperwork for the divorce stated that Cash had subjected her to "extreme cruelty" and "grievous mental suffering and anguish."

Vivian had wanted to make the marriage work, but due to Cash's increasing indifference, she couldn't take it anymore. After filing for divorce, Vivian still had no idea where her husband was or what had happened to him. Even the courts couldn't find him. He was supposed to attend a divorce hearing on August 22 of that year but failed to appear. It wasn't until August 29 that an attorney for Cash began to speak on the star's behalf.

Johnny and Vivian's daughter Kathy would later recall how frustrated Vivian was with her absentee husband. Kathy had inquired with her mom what life after the divorce would be like, and Vivian's sarcastic wit perfectly captured the moment when she responded, "Daddy's clothes would no longer be hanging in the closet." In other words, Cash was already absent from their lives; all Vivian was doing was making the separation official. The divorce was finalized on August 30, 1967. Cash didn't even try to fight it and allowed Vivian to walk away with full custody of the kids, $400 a month per child in child support, and promised to pay all of her legal fees for having to file for divorce in the first place.

After the divorce was official, Cash purchased a home in Hendersonville, Tennessee, just outside Nashville, where he tried to get his mind straight and refocus on music. It was an uphill battle, and due to the turmoil and strain he was under, Cash ended up failing to fulfill most of the gigs he was booked for that year. By this point, he was certainly down in the dumps. The only bright spot in his life now was June Carter.

Freed from his marriage to Vivian, it wasn't long before the two began to reconnect with each other. In a similar fashion to her previous intervention, June then began to once again intercede on Johnny's behalf, making it clear that if he truly wanted to be with her, he would have to quit taking drugs. June had Johnny see a psychiatrist named Nat Winston. Dr. Winston focused on having Cash work through his problems through therapy. It seemed to work, and by 1968, Johnny Cash was drug-free and on the rebound both in music as well as in his personal life.

First, he made his famous live album *Johnny Cash at Folsom Prison* in January. This record—in which one can hear real inmates cheering and shouting in between Johnny's songs—was an instant success. With his career on the upswing,

Cash then proposed marriage to June on February 22 while on stage in London, Ontario. Both recently divorced, they were married just one week after Cash made his proposal.

Yet even in the midst of this sudden surge of happiness, tragedy would strike. It was in August of 1968 that Johnny Cash's long-time band member, Luther Perkins, passed out on a sofa with a lit cigarette in hand. In what was one of the most horrible accidents imaginable, the sofa combusted into an inferno of flames and severely burned Perkins. The burns were so bad he died just a couple of days later.

As had been the case when he lost his brother in a tragic accident all those years ago, Cash was deeply disturbed by the death of Luther Perkins. As he would later confess, "A part of me died with Luther." Nevertheless, Cash knew that the show had to go on, and by the spring of 1969, he was on the road again to support his follow-up to Folsom Prison, recording *Johnny Cash at San Quentin*.

It was here that Cash showcased a new single called "A Boy Named Sue." The song is a rueful piece (actually written by Shel Silverstein, an author of children's books) about a boy who has had all kinds of problems in life simply because his father named him Sue. As the song lyrics explain, "Some gal would giggle and I'd turn red / And some guy'd laugh and I'd bust his head / I'll tell ya, life ain't easy for a boy named Sue." It's a humorous song for sure, and its wittiness struck a chord with many, allowing it to reach all the way to the number two spot on the singles' chart. The live album itself was quite a success as well, outdoing even the *Folsom Prison* piece.

It was on the heels of this success that ABC gave Cash his own show, the aptly named *Johnny Cash Show*. This variety show featured a wide variety of artists ranging from Bob Hope to Bob Dylan. The show was ultimately canceled in March of 1971, but it was well-received during its nearly three-year run. The show also helped to rehabilitate Johnny Cash's image. For those that were following the headlines of his drug addiction and messy divorce, seeing Johnny Cash seemingly healthy and happy on TV helped to reinvigorate his public persona.

Cash was indeed moving on with his life. By now, he and June had a son together—John Carter Cash—who was born in March of 1970. Unlike in the past, Johnny Cash desired to be a family man and was determined to be available for his young son, even though he had been largely absent from the lives of his other children.

Cash also became more involved with religion at this stage of his life. He befriended the televangelist Billy Graham and began to attend regular church services. Some of Johnny Cash's handlers cautioned him that he might alienate some of his fans by having too overtly Christian overtones, but Cash dismissed the notion by bluntly stating, "I don't have a career anymore. What I have now is a ministry."

Not holding back, Cash produced a religious film called *Gospel Road* with an accompanying soundtrack of gospel music. The film didn't do so well, but the album, which was released in 1973, did manage to get some traction on the country charts. It was all downhill from here, however, and by 1975, all of his album sales were flagging.

At this point, Columbia Records made the suggestion that Cash should try recording some newer material written by younger songwriters. This attempt to reinvigorate Cash's sinking ship met with failure. Johnny just wasn't selling records like he used to, and he was becoming increasingly depressed at his inability to make successful music. Down on his luck, he found himself falling back on his old ways. He quit church and began to delve back into drugs.

On August 16, 1977, Cash received another blow when he heard the news that Elvis Presley had died. Presley was a direct contemporary of Cash, and it was severely distressing to him that he had died depressed, alone, and addicted to drugs.

Cash's albums continued to fail meanwhile, with 1978's *Gone Girl* and 1980's *Rockabilly Blues* both failing to make any headway. Making matters even worse was a falling out that Cash had with his old surviving band member, Marshall Grant. Marshall, entirely fed up with Cash's behavior, left the band. But that wasn't all; he also ended up filing a lawsuit against Cash in 1980 for some $2.6 million dollars, over what Grant alleged to be a breach of contract and unwarranted slander. Cash, never one to stomach long, drawn-out court battles, ended up settling with Grant outside of the courtroom.

Cash was at this point in his life full throttle back into drugs, as was evidenced on November 10, 1983, when he was once again found fighting with inanimate objects. This time, his enemy was the wall of a hotel room. Completely out of his mind, Cash was convinced that the hotel had a fold-up bed in the wall—yet no such luxury existed. Nevertheless, Cash clawed at the wall until his hands were bloody and filled with wooden splinters. After the episode, he had to go to the hospital to have them taken out.

Shortly thereafter, Johnny Cash was admitted to the Betty Ford Center in California, where he spent several weeks sobering up. It was on the rebound from Betty Ford that Cash embarked on the next major epoch of his career by hooking up with Waylon Jennings, Willie Nelson, and Kris Kristofferson to form the supergroup called the Highwaymen. This collection of country legends would produce music together from 1985 to 1995, and within that ten-year span, they would release and tour for three full albums. Their biggest hit was the smash anthem "Highwayman," which was released in 1985.

Cash in the meantime pursued a wide variety of solo ventures throughout the late 1980s and early 1990s, but none of them seemed to pan out. It wasn't until the spring of 1993 that Johnny Cash finally made a breakthrough with the help of none other than the British pop star and U2 front man Bono. As it turns out, Bono was a big Cash fan and had asked him to record some vocals for the band's upcoming album *Zooropa*. It was through his dealings with Bono that Cash made the acquaintance of record producer Rick Rubin.

Rubin was famous for working with artists such as Run DMC, Slayer, and the Beastie Boys. Johnny Cash likely assumed someone like him wouldn't have much interest in his music, but Rubin most certainly did. Even though the pairing seemed unlikely, Cash was convinced to sign with Rubin's American Recordings label. The result was 1994's *American Recordings* album which had Cash playing an acoustic guitar and singing stripped-down songs. This album would render hits such as "Drive On," and the album itself did quite well. The follow-up piece *Unchained* was also a success and won a Grammy in 1998 for Best Country Album.

Johnny's health began to decline shortly thereafter, however, causing him to cancel most of his concerts. It seemed that the old highwayman was finally at the end of his road, but nevertheless, Johnny Cash would prove that he still had a few more surprises left for his fans.

Conclusion

By the year 2000, Cash's health was in serious decline, and his public appearances became few and far between. Behind the scenes, he still kept working on his music. He took his time, and when he was up to it, Cash went to the studio to record. He chose a wide variety of songs to work with, but it was a song suggested by Rick Rubin that really seemed to come together for him.

That song was "Hurt," originally written by Trent Reznor of the alternative rock band Nine Inch Nails. At first glance, Johnny Cash covering a Nine Inch Nails song might almost seem comical, but once Cash got to work with it, the results were incredible. Reznor's song was a sad and somber piece about someone attaining greatness only to realize they've lost everything and everyone that ever mattered to them. It was this sentiment that Cash truly seemed to capture when his old, weathered voice sings the words, "What have I become? My sweetest friend / Everyone I know goes away in the end." Johnny Cash then reinforces Reznor's bleak chorus, "And you could have it all / My empire of dirt / I will let you down / I will make you hurt."

Even though this is indeed a cover song, Cash did such a remarkable job with it that he almost made it his, and it became his last smash hit. The video that was made of Cash performing it proved just as stunning. Even more haunting perhaps was the fact that Johnny Cash died just a short time after the cover was released. The song came out in March of 2003, and Cash passed away in the early morning hours of September 12, making the image of Cash at the end of his life singing the words of "Hurt" the last thing that many would remember.

Bibliography

Alexander, John M. (2018). *The Man in Song: A Discographic Biography of Johnny Cash*.

Cash, Johnny (1998). *Johnny Cash: The Autobiography*.

Cash, Vivian; Sharpsteen, Ann (2007). *I Walked the Line: My Life with Johnny*.

D'Ambrosio, Antonio (2009). *A Heartbeat and a Guitar: Johnny Cash and the Making of Bitter Tears*.

Edwards, Leigh (2009). *Johnny Cash and the Paradox of American Identity*.

Hilburn, Robert (2013). *Johnny Cash: The Life*.

Streissguth, Michael (2006). *Johnny Cash: The Biography*.

Willett, Edward (2010). *Johnny Cash: The Man in Black*.

Made in the USA
Middletown, DE
23 January 2023

22853872R00033